Sanctuary

Steven Eastlake

BookLeaf Publishing

India | USA | UK

Presentation by *BookLeaf Publishing*

Web: www.bookleafpub.com

E-mail: info@bookleafpub.com

ISBN: 9789358314212

First edition 2023

DEDICATION

To my Wife, thank you for everything. We love you dearly.

ACKNOWLEDGEMENT

I'd like to thank whatever force it was that made me pick up a pen whilst working a twelve-hour shift one day, and begin to scribble down my thoughts. I remember it vividly. It was counseling without me knowing it.
I would like to thank my Mother and Father for their constant support, not only for myself but for my family too.

Heavenly feather

So gentle does the feather
Journey to the ground
Before being kicked back up
By a herd of screaming children
Running round and round

Off it goes again
With not a care
Effortlessly it sails
In rhythm with the air

Content to go where it is shown
The endless power of the wind
Allowing it to roam

O to sit upon its spine
And be taken for a ride
The hectic noise of the world below
Disappears as we soar mountain high

Where has this beauty been
So elegant so clean
When will the wind let go of its guest
And let it come to rest

Settling down it nestles in
O look a feather
As it's spotted by a human

We have had a visitor they say
As they look to heaven

Life

Money gets you down
Love gives you the runaround
Time it flies by
Youth disappears in the blink of an eye

Bills pull you under
Best friends crossing each other
The government always telling you lies
People talking to others they despise

Life pulls you into the riptide
Takes you under and spins you around
Spits you out upon the shore
Stands over you
To see if you want more

But we will fight
Yea we will fight
For the right to live this life
Yes you can hit me, knock me to the floor
Stand over me
I'll come back for more
Yea I'll be back for more.

COALVILLE

Coalville children of today
Will never truly know the Coalville way
Partly because of change, partly their fault
And now the real Coalville is locked away in the
vault

The water fights through the streets
Late nights in the Blythe playing darts for the
meat
Building dens and Wembley doubles
Pals getting you through teenage troubles

Brook jumping for hours in a day
All the other kids wanted to come to Coalville to
play
Walking free, yes free from street to street
A welcoming face whoever you meet

Coalville scrubbers, rainbow city
We didn't care what they said
To us it was pretty
And they'd get a crack round the head

The harsh times
The strikes

The police lights
The fights
Sleepless nights
Loss of life

Calling your elders by their second name
Mates sticking together when someone's to
blame
Bikes down the fields, our fields of dreams
Coalville as we know it ripped apart at the seems

There are those who looked in
And may disagree
But you have to wonder
Were they of true Coalville pedigree

Reminisce and reminisce
Just in case there are bits you miss
As nostalgia kicks in, as hard as you try
You'll get a lump in your throat and a tear in
your eye

It's official I am sad to say
Those special days are now so far away
The Coalville spirit that lifted us all so high
Is now with our loved ones up in the sky.

Weekend millionaire

You work a 9 to 5 like all the rest
Always thought you were the best
You don't do anything to change the world
So I don't know what you think you're owed

Always looking down your nose
Got to have the best clothes
Always got to look the part
Like you just walked off a yacht

Don't make me look bad for you to look good
Treat people how you know you should
Flashing your cash for all to see
Offer of a drink yet to be seen

You come running when you're down and out
Dig up that money you talk about
We all know you talk the talk
We will find out if you can walk the walk

You're a beer-drinking champagne lover
Work a 9 to 5 like every other
It doesn't matter how you look or wear your hair
We all know you're just a weekend millionaire.

Evil mind

Those crocodile tears
That you shed
Turn to ice
With the thoughts in your head.

That false pretty smile
Falls away at the sides
Turns to a scowl
The devil comes to mind

That gentle touch
Becomes firmer in your clutch
The affection in your caress
Becomes an ugly violent mess

Your softly spoken words
Don't take long to hurt
The poison from your tongue
Sets in before too long

There's nowhere to hide
From the evil in your mind
Praying on any weakness
That you may find.

Sanctuary

Found you during a winter walk
Three of us but not much talk
Seen you off the beaten track
Stories told seen the aftermath

There you were standing all alone
So far away but felt like home
As I took a step inside
It was clear you had been so many's shrine

Made emotions hard to hide
Made words hard to find

The candle light lay me down
Thoughts flooding in from all around
Whispering prayers I should of already said
Did you know how much I cared
The thought you didn't
Makes me scared

As I left I looked behind
Found some answers I could not find
Pulled to the crooked door
My heart strings they were torn

The candle light faded away
In my heart you will stay

You were there for me
In my time of need
You were there for me
My own piece of sanctuary.

Got to get it right

As I take a look through the window at my life, it
seems
The grey clouds have taken over my sky and it seems
The rain always hits me in my face, it never seems to
miss
And the wind blows me everywhere like I'm not even
there
And I can't see through this fog
Where did I go wrong.

As I take a look at my life through my dreams
The bright blue sky hangs over the grass bank by the
stream
I feel the hot sunshine and smell the pretty flowers
Taste the cheap red wine and laugh away the hours
Now and then we get the odd shower
But they never last long
Where did I go wrong

Where is the life that I have dreamt of
I can't see it through my window
Won't you tell me where it was I went wrong
I've got to get it right.

Sunshine

When you go to bed
I look to descend
As if I am ready
To rest my head

But off I go all around
Until I get to the other end
Ready to greet
The tired eyes
That crack open
As I rise

Hanging over you
Like a comfort blanket
Bringing warmth and joy
There I will stay
For all of the day
While you work and play

When I see you are weary
Your eyes beginning to close
Like a lighthouse
Slowly blinking out at sea
I will settle you down
But I'm not going to bed

I'm off again
Back to the other end

Not to worry
I will see you again
Your most joyful alarm clock
Until the seasons change.

Master

A sulking child chin cleaning the floor
Firing bullet after bullet of foul language
At the teacher before unhanging the door

It's not fair, it's not right
kicking the wall like a mule
With all of there mite

Everyone telling me what to do
They don't own me
And neither do you

Listen child you think this is rough
When the big boss comes calling
Then it gets tough

Once you step out and in to his land
He is the giant
And you are in the palm of his hand

Let me introduce you
To the real master

Hi I'm life
I hope that you are ready
This roller coaster just gets faster.

Time

They say that time waits for no man
Was there ever a truer phrase
Do we get out of each minute
What we can
Making the most of these precious days

The haunting sound of the ticking clock
Reminding us of yet another second
That we have lost
Sprint as you may, you will never catch
Another lost day

Embrace your time
Sip it up like a fine wine
Make hay while the sun shines
Yes it's ok to stop and take it in
Every once in a while

Take out the battery from the watch
Unplug the dreaded alarm clock
It can't be stopped it's still there
Ticking away
With the change in the air

Do not regret time that has gone by
Or you will miss a lot more
In the blink of an eye

Make memories, be kind
Educate yourself and of course
Unwind
Time can be your best friend
Always there for you and on your side.

I don't want to forget the past

I don't want to forget the past
When the buildings were dreary and ugly but
made to last
I don't want to forget the past
When the days seemed longer and the blue skies
would last
No I do don't want to forget the past

What's wrong with being nostalgic anyway?
About the good old days
Get out of my head and out of my way
I don't want to forget the past

Be sure to be careful as you walk
Through the smoke screen to the new better days
There's no space for you if you can't talk the
talk
The days are short
And the skies are grey anyway

I don't want to forget the past
Those days went way too fast
Leave me behind
And I will find
My way

Leave me behind
And I will find
My way

Those days were golden, please do not take them
away
Don't try to brainwash me
Those days will go down in history
Just you wait and see.

The lonely tree

The lonely tree stands ruggedly
In the abandoned field
Not even a sheep
To itch its ancient bark

Trembling in the crisp winter wind
That whistles through its fragile branches
Its bones creaking as it passes
Begging for no more

With not a leaf
To guard it from the enemy
They leave to hide in the comfort
Of the clumpy grass
taking shelter
Waiting for it to pass

Its skin with knots the size of elephant ears
Listens intently for any visitor it may get
Only the harrowing squawk of the pearly black
crow
Starts to grow, as it nears

Menacingly it lands gently,
Silence falls down

Used as a lookout, still stands the tree
With not a whisper of wind
Taking comfort in the company.

Every day is a battle

Every day is a battle
Not just a fight
Another war around the corner
As another week passes by

There's so much more
Than what I said
If you could only see
Inside my head

No more alcohol for me
No more alcohol for me
No more alcohol for me
I'm sinking down
And I'm down on my knees

When you look at me
What do you see
Don't be kind
I need your honesty

Turn the negative into positive
Rising to my feet
I feel new energy
Rushing through my body

No more alcohol for me
No more alcohol for me
No more alcohol for me
I'm sinking down
And I'm down on my knees.

Us and them

Manipulated, now used as bait
Before you switch to the other side
Think hard, just wait

Don't forget their twisted lies
How they strangled your insides

Remember where you are from
Just the other day
Thought of as scum

Why would they want you on their team
You're doing their dirty work
While they take the cream

Give them your vote
Give into freedom
This is not how it should be run

Soon the divide with be far and wide
Us and them
And you will be something
On the bottom of their shoe again.

Special one

Like a bun in the homeliest of ovens
Nurtured and tended to by the most
Thorough of bakers

Watching you rise
With an attentive eye
And a mind that was wise
Carefully carefully
With our most precious prize

The time came to take you out
Your cry music to our ears
The warmth in our hands
Made us melt
Our senses fought to take you in
Our eyes widen as we inhale
To kiss your soft skin

Nine months we waited for you to bake
My god how good you look, smell and taste
Proudly showing you off to everyone
The birth of our special one.

A parent's sacrifice

If the iron is so painfully hot to touch
Then why does my mother hold it so much

If the spade makes my father's back ache
Then why does he dig
Each morning he wakes

Of course it is for my brother and I
That our parents make this sacrifice.

The Athlete

The first to hear the bird sing
To see the sun as it peeps over the horizon
Looking to see who is about
Before it stretches out into the morning sky

Sending the first shock wave into the earth
With the pounding of the foot
Footprint left in a carpet of untouched frost
Breath leaving clouds in the still silent air
Like a locomotive taking off on its first
Journey of the day

How does the water lie so calm, like glass
Until entering it like an arrow
Breaking its barrier, churning it up
Into a storm with every pull
Dragging your tired body

When the others leave for home
The grass dares to try and stand
Peeling itself from the sticky mud
Only to be flattened again
By your persistence.

Remember to love

Talk about regret
Talk about forgive and forget
Talk about the first
And last time you met

See a story unfolding
Unfolding inside of your mind
See it in the future
See it back in time

What a story it was
A hero, a villain
A love story of joy and tears
Real life with happiness and fears

Dark times
Don't elude anyone
Trying to identify
As someone

Whatever your identity
Make sure you are free
Small-mindedness never prevails
It just crucifies people with nails

Be humble be kind
But don't give away everything
That's behind those eyes
Be firm when needed
And for others be strong
Be big enough
To say when you're wrong

Take your chance
At first glance
At the second time of asking
It may of gone packing

Make sure you don't
Look back with regret
Make memories
You will never forget

Try all the things you want
And are able to do
Take risks
And be sure to see things through

Most importantly
Remember to love
If you don't then
Forget all of the above.

Brave soul

I never knew a brave soul
Without any anguish
Flustered with emotion
Speaking without thought
Not hiding but stepping up
When they ought

Have you ever known such a brave soul?

The cold, my old friend

The cold is my old friend
Showing up when I'm alone
Gives me the harsh truth
That gets right to your gut
Finding all of your niggles
And weaknesses
Reminding you that the warmth
Was comforting indeed.

Purpose

What is the purpose I hear you say?
Striving to be a better version of oneself
In this beautifully difficult world
Come what may

To succeed in our ambitions
Chasing our dreams
Whilst maintaining our footing
No giving up
Not for nothing

Think carefully before we speak
Not everyone is strong
The words of a clown
Can be so weak
But can knock even the strongest down

Doing what we can for the good
Stern when needed
Look after yourself you should
But always followed with
Compassion, loyalty
And love.